ROMANS

FACTS ● THINGS TO MAKE ● ACTIVITIES

NICOLA BAXTER

Watts Books

London ● New York ● Sydney

© Watts Books 1992
   This edition 1995
Watts Books
96 Leonard Street
London EC2A 4RH

Franklin Watts
14 Mars Road
Lane Cove
NSW 2066

UK ISBN: 0 7496 0762 9 (hardback)
           0 7496 1511 7 (paperback)

Editor: Hazel Poole
Designed by: Sally Boothroyd
Artwork by: Nigel Longden
Photography by: Chris Fairclough
Additional picture research by: Juliet Duff

The publishers would like to thank
Kirsty Witkowska and Andy Witkowski
for their participation with the
photographs in this book.

A CIP catalogue record for this book
is available from the British Library.

Printed in the United Kingdom

CONTENTS

THE STORY OF THE ROMANS

Nearly two thousand years ago, the Romans ruled a huge empire. Large parts of Europe, Africa and the Middle East were under Roman control. Some of the names that the Romans gave to the countries they conquered are still used today.

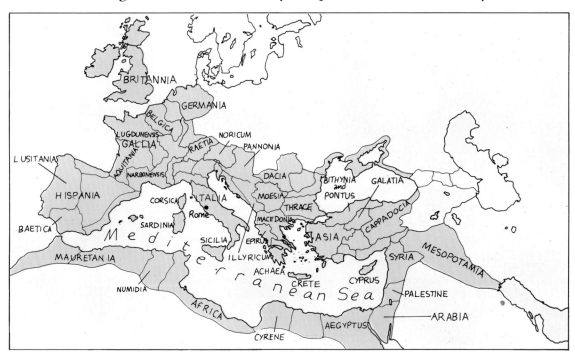

The Romans changed the lives of people in all parts of their empire. They took their own language and ideas to every country. They built roads and towns. They made people obey Roman laws and pay taxes, but usually they let the people they conquered choose their own religions.

Jesus was born in a part of the Roman Empire called Palestine. We use the date of His birth to describe when things happened. BC means "before Christ" and AD stands for *anno Domini.* That is "in the year of our Lord" in Latin, the language of the Romans. AD 100 is 100 years after the birth of Jesus. The Romans are often mentioned in the New Testament.

We know a lot about the Romans because they left behind books, pictures, buildings and other things that we can look at today. Some of what we know about the Romans has been discovered by archaeologists, who dig carefully at Roman sites to find traces from the time of the Romans.

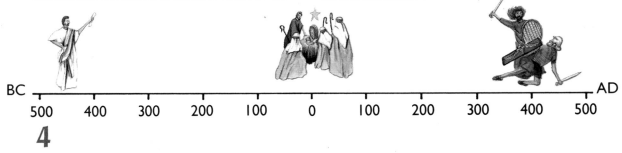

BC | | | | | | | | | AD
500   400   300   200   100   0   100   200   300   400   500

WHERE DID THE ROMANS COME FROM?

The Romans took their name from the city of Rome, in Italy. We do not know very much about the early days of Rome, but the Romans themselves loved to tell stories about how things began. They said that a man called Romulus gave the city its name. When Romulus and his twin brother Remus were born, their uncle had them thrown into the River Tiber. The babies were rescued and raised by a female wolf. Later, Romulus built the first city of Rome by the river and became its first king.

▲ *This statue of Romulus, Remus and the wolf can be seen in Rome.*

THE REPUBLIC

It seems that the Romans were ruled by kings for over 250 years, but by about 500 BC they decided that it was dangerous for one man to have all the power. A republic was formed. This meant that the rulers were chosen by the people themselves by voting at an election. This kind of government is called a democracy. In Roman times, women were not allowed to vote and some people, called slaves, had no rights at all.

The most important jobs in the republic were done by the consuls and the senate. The two consuls led the country and the army. The senate was made up of senators. At first there were 100 senators, but later there were as many as 600. They gave advice to the consuls and had a lot of power themselves.

THE ROMAN EMPIRE

Soon the Romans began to conquer nearby lands. By 130 BC they ruled all of Italy and Greece and most of Spain. Many Romans became very rich, but the lives of the poor people did not improve. People found it hard to agree on how to solve the problems this caused. In 27 BC, one man took control of all the Roman lands and people. He was given the name Augustus and became the first Roman emperor. This was the beginning of the Roman Empire.

Of course, the Roman Empire did not last for ever. You can read about how it ended on page 28.

A ROMAN TOWN

In all the lands they conquered, the Romans built towns that they could feel at home in. Each town was built to a plan. The Romans liked things to be well-organised and orderly. When they conquered Greek cities, they noticed that the streets were laid out in a criss-cross pattern, called a grid. The Romans liked this pattern and used it in their own towns. Often there were two main streets that divided the town. Smaller streets led off these at right angles.

Every large town contained the buildings that you see on these pages. A Roman town in Africa could look very like a Roman town in Britain or Greece. Seeing what buildings a Roman town had in it tells us a lot about how the Romans lived.

The *thermae*, or bath-houses, were not only places for washing, but somewhere to meet friends and spend spare time. Large bath-houses had restaurants, games rooms, snack bars and even libraries. Baths ranged from very hot, where people sat round as in a sauna, to very cold. Men and women either had separate bath-houses or used the same one at different times.

The *amphitheatre* was where shows were put on. Some of these seem cruel to us today. People could watch wild animals fighting each other or attacking people. There were also gladiator fights where two men would fight each other until one of them was dead.

Many towns had walls around them with gates to let people and animals in. Just like today, there were often traffic jams! Some places tried to avoid this by only allowing carts into the town at night.

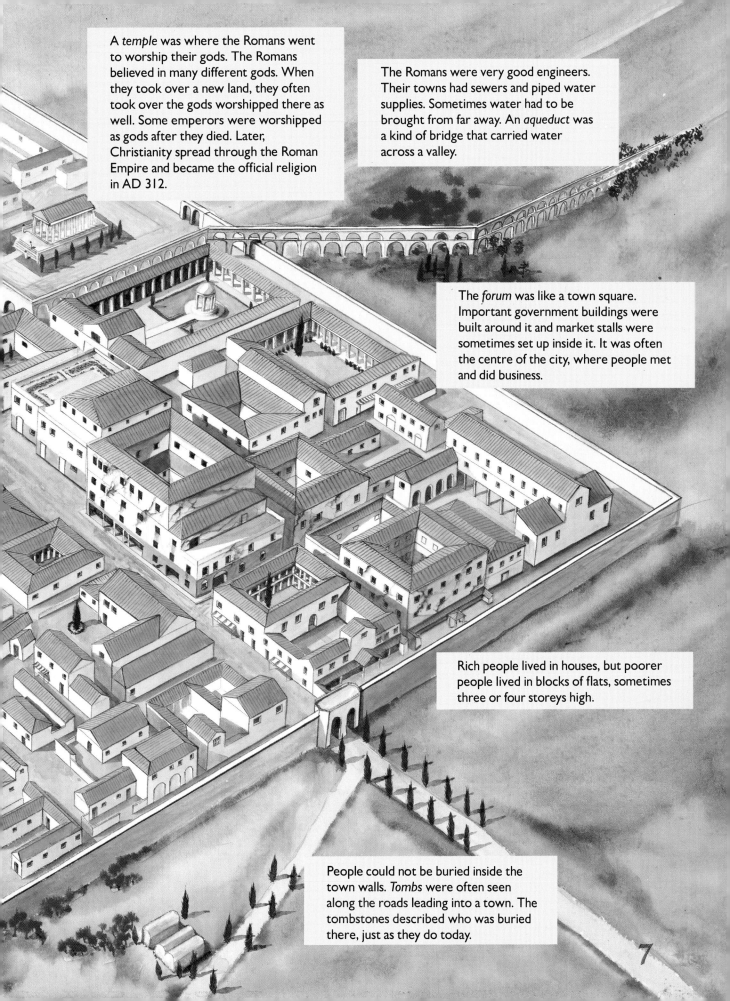

A *temple* was where the Romans went to worship their gods. The Romans believed in many different gods. When they took over a new land, they often took over the gods worshipped there as well. Some emperors were worshipped as gods after they died. Later, Christianity spread through the Roman Empire and became the official religion in AD 312.

The Romans were very good engineers. Their towns had sewers and piped water supplies. Sometimes water had to be brought from far away. An *aqueduct* was a kind of bridge that carried water across a valley.

The *forum* was like a town square. Important government buildings were built around it and market stalls were sometimes set up inside it. It was often the centre of the city, where people met and did business.

Rich people lived in houses, but poorer people lived in blocks of flats, sometimes three or four storeys high.

People could not be buried inside the town walls. *Tombs* were often seen along the roads leading into a town. The tombstones described who was buried there, just as they do today.

A ROMAN VILLA

A villa was the country home of a wealthy family. Villas were first designed to suit the warm weather of Italy. The hall, or *atrium*, in the middle was open to the sky. There was often a small pool in the centre. The overhanging roof gave cool, shady places to sit in the open air, out of the hot sun. The marble floors were cool in hot weather, too.

When the Romans built villas in other, colder parts of their empire, they had to change them a little to suit the weather. A heating system under the floor kept the villas warm, and bigger windows let more sunshine inside.

The country villa of a very rich Roman might have been built in the middle of a huge estate. This one is surrounded by woods, fields and orchards. The villa also has a carefully planned garden with flower beds and pools. ▼

MAKE A ROMAN VILLA

You will need: two cereal packets of the same size ● pencil ● sticky tape ● scissors ● paper ● glue ● corrugated cardboard ● string ● large cardboard box ● trimming knife ● poster paints and brushes ● blue plasticine.

Ask an adult to help you with this, as the knife blade will be sharp!

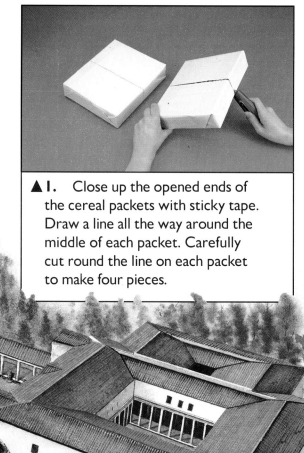

▲1. Close up the opened ends of the cereal packets with sticky tape. Draw a line all the way around the middle of each packet. Carefully cut round the line on each packet to make four pieces.

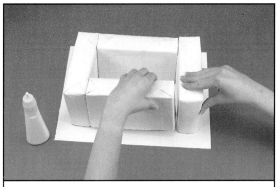

▲ **2.** Turn the pieces upside down and glue them together to make a rectangle. This makes your villa walls. Covering the walls with plain paper will make them easier to paint later. Cut a piece of card from the cardboard box, big enough for your villa to stand on.

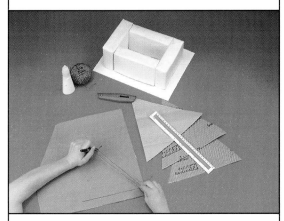

▲ **3.** On the smooth side of the corrugated cardboard, draw a line 2cm longer than the outside wall of your villa. Make a loop of string the same length as your line. Hold one end of the loop at the end of the line and put a pencil at the other end of the loop. With the pencil, make a mark above the line in the middle. Do the same on the other side. The place where the marks cross makes the top of a triangle. Join up the sides and cut out the triangle. Make three more triangles to fit the other walls. Make sure the corrugated lines run the same way on all of them.

▲ **4.** Draw two lines on the back of one of your triangles. Cut along the top line. Run the points of your scissors along the bottom line so that it will fold easily. This makes one piece of roof. Do the same with the other triangles, making sure that the lines are in exactly the same place.

5. Use sticky tape inside to join the four pieces of roof together. Stand the roof on top of the villa.

6. Now have fun painting and decorating your villa! Cut out doors and windows where you like. You can make a pool in the middle with a little strip of corrugated cardboard and fill it with blue plasticine to look like water.

EATING AND DRINKING

Just as rich people had bigger houses than poorer people, there were differences in the food they had to eat, too. This dinner party is being given by a very wealthy man. His guests lie on comfortable couches instead of sitting on chairs. They eat with their fingers.

The man giving the party has a lot of slaves to do all the work. They are like servants, but they are owned by their master and have no rights. They cannot leave if they do not like the work, or do anything without their master's permission. Some slaves bring the food and drink. Others wipe the guests' fingers. Slaves also play music and dance to entertain the guests.

A rich man would try to impress his guests by serving very special food and wine. It might include ingredients from far away, such as spices from Asia. The Romans used lots of herbs and spices and ate animals that we do not think of as food, such as dormice! There was no sugar, so honey was used to make things sweet.

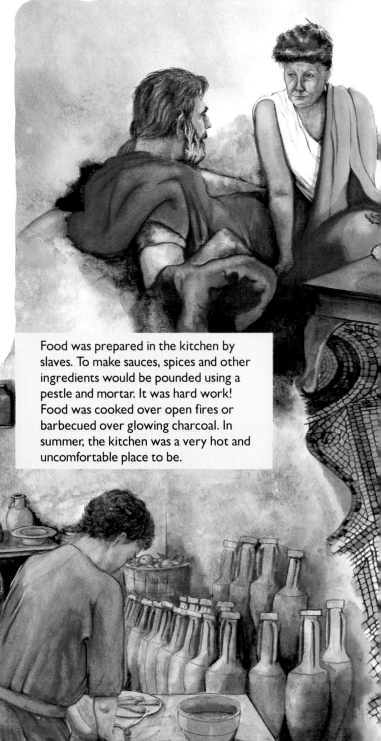

Food was prepared in the kitchen by slaves. To make sauces, spices and other ingredients would be pounded using a pestle and mortar. It was hard work! Food was cooked over open fires or barbecued over glowing charcoal. In summer, the kitchen was a very hot and uncomfortable place to be.

Poor people could not afford meat or fish or fine wine. They ate mainly bread or a kind of porridge made from wheat. Most of them did not have kitchens in their small flats. If they wanted hot food, they bought it from one of the many snack bars in the town.

Wine was stored in pointed pots called *amphorae*. Indoors they had to be propped against a wall. Outside they were sometimes buried up to their necks in the ground to keep the wine inside cool.

ROMAN ART

The Romans loved to fill their towns and homes with beautiful things. From different parts of the empire came precious stones, marble for carving, and gold and silver. There were many skilled craftsmen, sculptors, jewellers and painters. Luckily, many lovely pictures, statues and ornaments have been found buried in the ruins of Roman towns.

▲ *Part of Constantine's huge statue.*

Statues were very popular. Some were small enough to stand on a table. Some were life-size. Some people had *huge* statues of themselves made to show how important they were. This giant head was part of a statue of Emperor Constantine the Great. Turn to page 27 to find out how to make your own statue.

Today we hang pictures on our walls, but the Romans liked to paint pictures on the walls themselves. The artist would begin to paint while the plaster on the walls was still wet. This made the colours very bright and helped them to last a long time—even until today! All kinds of scenes were painted. Sometimes they showed a garden or some columns that looked so real they made a room seem larger than it actually was.

Mosaics were also very popular. They were made up of tiny pieces of stone pressed into wet plaster to make a pattern or picture. The more complicated the pattern was, the smaller the pieces had to be. Up to one million pieces might be needed to make one square metre of mosaic! Some mosaics were useful as well as beautiful. This one was found at the doorway to a home. The words mean: Beware of the dog!

▶ *This "Beware of the dog" mosaic was found at the doorway of a Roman home in Pompeii.*

Make your own Mosaic

▲**1.** First wash your eggshells carefully in some soapy water. Try not to break them yet! Let them dry and then paint them with different coloured poster paints.

2. Decide what picture or pattern you would like to make, and draw it on the card. You can copy a picture from this book or make up one of your own.

▲**3.** Spread some PVA over a little piece of the card. Break off some pieces of shell of the colour you want to use, and press them gently on to the glue. Like the Romans, you can decide how big your pieces need to be. But don't make them too small or it will take you a long time to finish your mosaic! Only put PVA on a small part at a time so that the glue does not dry while you are choosing your pieces.

4. You could hang your finished mosaic on the wall. Imagine how long it must have taken the Romans to cover a whole floor with mosaic!

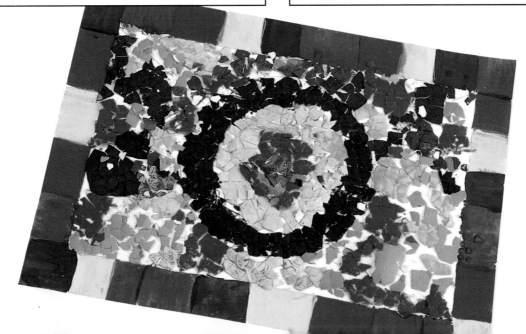

13

SPORT AND SPECTACLES

Ordinary people couldn't afford to have mosaics on their floors, but they could go out to see a show. Often these were free, paid for by a wealthy man who wanted the people to support him. Many of these shows seem dangerous or cruel to us today, but the Romans enjoyed them very much.

▲ *A charioteer races with four horses.*

ANIMAL FIGHTS

Animals were brought from all over the empire. Lions, bears, zebras, elephants and giraffes were made to fight each other in the arena. There are even reports of the amphitheatre being flooded so that crocodiles and hippopotamuses could be shown. Sometimes the animals were made to attack people. Not all Romans liked this kind of show.

SPORTS

Romans thought it was important to have a healthy body. Running, wrestling and javelin-throwing were popular sports for men. At the bath-houses men also used weights to help build their muscles.

CHARIOT RACING

This exciting sport usually took place at a special race-track. A lightweight chariot was drawn by two or four horses. The drivers wore helmets and padded clothes, but even so they were often badly hurt, especially when the chariot turned the corner at the end of the track. There were four teams: the Reds, Blues, Greens and Whites. People supported one team and cheered on its drivers—just like supporting a football team today.

GLADIATOR FIGHTS

Gladiators were usually slaves from different parts of the empire. Often they had been captured in wars. They carried different weapons, but were carefully matched so that the fight lasted a long time. Usually the fight ended when one of the gladiators was killed, but sometimes a gladiator who had fought very bravely would be allowed to live.

▲ *Many animals were killed at shows.*

MAKE A VICTOR'S WREATH

The winner at the games or races was called the victor. He was often given a prize and a wreath of laurel leaves to show he was the winner. Why not make your own wreath?

You will need: some pipe cleaners ● ● paper or card ● glue ● paints or felt-tip pens.

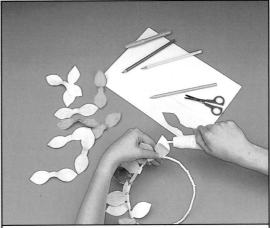

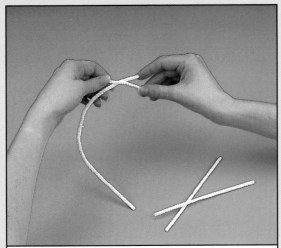

▲ **1.** Twist some pipe cleaners together to make an open circle that fits round your head.

2. Trace the pattern below on to paper or thin card. You will need to do this about 20 times. You could use green paper or colour the leaves with paints or felt-tip pens.

▲ **3.** Cut out each pair of leaves and put glue on the plain side. Fold the pairs in half around the pipe cleaner and press them firmly together to make one leaf. Do this all the way round the pipe cleaner. Some leaves should point upwards and some downwards. You can curl them round a pencil if you want them to look real.

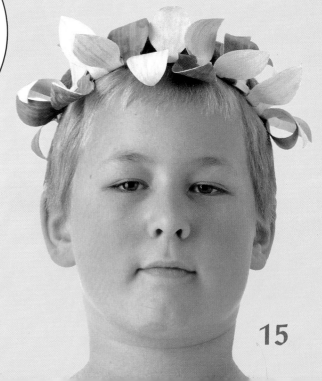

ROMAN THEATRE

Theatre was something else that the Romans learnt from the Greeks. At first they only put on Greek plays, but later Roman plays were written and special theatres were built. Like Greek theatres, they were D-shaped and larger ones could hold up to 30,000 people.

Only rich and powerful people had seats near the stage. Poorer people had seats further away, high up at the back. The actors wore bright masks and costumes so that everyone could see who they were meant to be. The masks also funnelled the actor's voice, just as a megaphone does, so that he could be heard throughout the theatre.

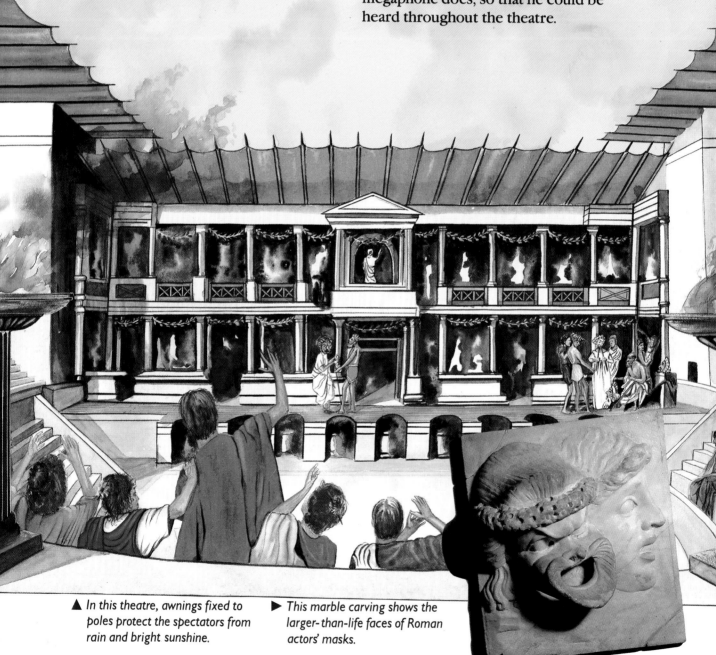

▲ *In this theatre, awnings fixed to poles protect the spectators from rain and bright sunshine.*

▶ *This marble carving shows the larger-than-life faces of Roman actors' masks.*

MAKE YOUR OWN MASK

Ask a grown-up to help you with this, as the knife blade will be sharp!

1. Tear the old newspapers into small pieces and soak them in water overnight in the plastic container.

2. Mash up the paper a bit more with your fingers. Then squeeze out as much water as possible and mix in some PVA. Add enough so that the paper can be modelled into different shapes.

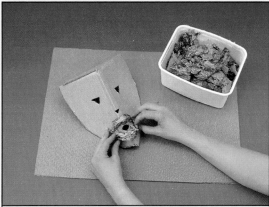

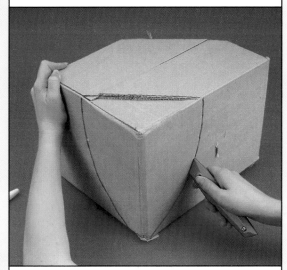

▲3. Cut out the corner of the cardboard box in a mask shape. Make it a bit bigger than your face so that it will show up from a distance.

4. Cut out two holes about 3cm wide for your eyes, and a slightly bigger hole for your mouth. Then draw on some features like eyebrows, nose and lips. Again, remember to make these as large as possible—they can be much bigger than the holes you have cut.

▲5. Use your paper mixture to build up features on the mask. When you have finished, leave it somewhere warm to dry.

6. Paint your mask in bright colours. To wear your mask, make two little holes at the sides and thread the elastic through.

YOUNG ROMANS

The head of a Roman family was the father. When a new baby was born, it was put on the floor in front of him. The father picked the baby up as a sign that it was now part of the family.

When the baby was named, a lucky charm was put around its neck. This was called a *bulla*. It was meant to keep the baby safe from harm.

TOYS

Some toys from Roman times have been found. Roman children had dolls and little models of people and animals to play with. They also played board games using dice. Outdoor games using balls and hoops were popular, too.

SCHOOL

Children whose parents were quite rich went to school when they were about six. They learnt to read and write and studied the writing of famous Roman authors. Some boys went to another school when they were eleven. Here they learnt more subjects, such as history, geography, astronomy, music and Greek. The Romans thought highly of Greek learning, so it was important to be able to read books by Greek writers.

GROWING UP

In Roman times, people often got married when they were very young. A girl might be 12 and a boy 14. A girl would offer her toys to the gods as a sign that she was no longer a child. Boys usually had a special ceremony when they were 14 to show that they were now grown up. They took off their childish clothes and *bulla* and put on adult clothes, including a toga.

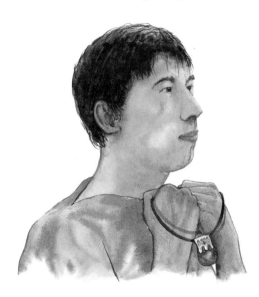

Usually a boy or girl could not choose the person they were to marry. Their parents and relatives arranged it for them. A Roman bride wore a white dress and a red veil. The bridegroom carried the bride over the threshold of their new home. This was so that the bride did not stumble—that would have been thought very unlucky.

WRITING LATIN

Latin was the language of the Romans. They spoke it in all parts of their empire. But Latin did not die out when the Roman Empire ended. It became an important language of learning. The Bible was translated into Latin, and for hundreds of years important documents were always written in Latin.

You may already know some Latin words! Many English words come from Latin, with only small changes. Languages such as Italian and Spanish are even closer to Latin than English is. You have probably used some of the letters below without knowing that they are the first letters or abbreviations of Latin words. Do you know what they mean?

PS	*post scriptum*
NB	*nota bene*
am	*ante meridiem*
pm	*post meridiem*

The answers are on page 29.

▲ Can you find any Roman names in this Latin carving?

In Roman times, important documents were written on scrolls. These were long rolls of a kind of paper, often 10 metres long. The paper was made from reeds and was called papyrus.

Papyrus was expensive, so children learning to write used writing tablets so that it didn't matter if they made a mistake. The tablets were made of wood with melted wax poured into the middle. When the wax was hard, children used a special pointed stick called a *stylus* to scratch letters on it. To use the tablet again, they used the flat end of the stick to smooth out the wax.

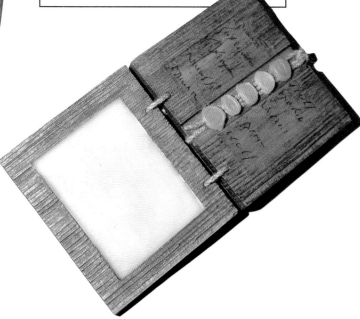

▲ This writing tablet could be closed up like a book.

MAKE A WRITING TABLET

You can use plasticine to make a writing tablet that works in the same way as a wax tablet.

You will need: a pencil and ruler ● a strong cardboard box ● a trimming knife ● glue ● some plasticine ● a rolling pin ● poster paints or felt-tip pens ● a modelling tool.

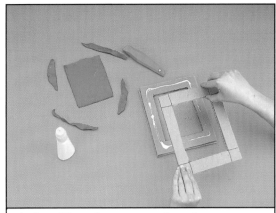

1. Draw three rectangles of the same size on the cardboard box and ask a grown-up to help cut them out carefully with the knife.

▲2. Put your ruler along the edge of one of the rectangles and draw a line. Do the same thing on the other sides. Cut along the lines with the knife so that you make a window. Do the same thing with *one* of the other rectangles.

3. Roll out the plasticine until it is about half a centimetre thick. Put one of the cardboard windows over the plasticine and use it as a guide to cut out a piece of plasticine the same size as the window.

▲4. Glue the pieces of card together as in the picture, and put the plasticine rectangle in the middle. You can put a little bit of extra plasticine round the edges to make sure it doesn't fall out.

5. Decorate the edges of your writing tablet with paints or felt tips. Use the modelling tool as a *stylus*. You can write with the pointed end and smooth out your writing again with the flat end.

DRESS LIKE A ROMAN

Roman men and women wore all sorts of different clothes. It depended on where they came from, how rich they were, and what kind of work they did.

The kinds of clothes we most often think of the Romans as wearing are those you see below. They would be worn by fairly wealthy people, probably living in a town or city.

The woman is wearing a *stola* with a *palla* over it. A *stola* was quite a simple dress, often fastened with brooches at the shoulders. The *palla* was a large shawl that could be worn in different ways. Both of them might be made of beautiful coloured materials.

The man is wearing a tunic with a *toga* over it. The *toga* was a very big half-circle of cloth that had to be carefully folded and arranged.

A STOLA AND PALLA

1. Fold one sheet in half lengthwise. Hold it up to your shoulders and ask a friend to mark where it reaches the floor. Cut across the sheet at that point.

2. Sew up the side of the sheet, but leave the top and bottom open.

You will need: two old single sheets ● scissors ● needle and thread ● string or cord ● scraps of coloured card and paper ● glue ● sticky tape ● safety pins ● a friend to help you!

▲3. Make some brooches by using sticky tape to fix safety pins to pieces of card cut into shapes. Decorate them with coloured paper shapes.

4. Use the brooches to pin together the top edge of your stola – but leave a space for your head!

5. Put on your stola. Tie two pieces of cord or string around you, and pull the stola up over them a bit.

6. The second sheet makes your palla. Drape it around yourself however you like, or look through this book for some ideas.

A TUNIC AND TOGA

You will need: a large T-shirt ● an old single sheet ● a felt-tip pen ● string ● scissors ● a large open space ● someone to help you!

1. Spread out the sheet on the floor. Find the middle of one of the long sides and make a small mark with a felt-tip pen. Cut a piece of string the same length as from the mark to the end of the sheet, but add a few more centimetres for making a knot.

▲**2.** Tie one end of the string to a felt-tip pen, and ask a friend to hold the other end at the mark on the sheet. Very slowly and carefully, stretch out the string and let the felt-tip pen mark the sheet as you move round. You will draw a half-circle. Cut along the line to make your toga.

3. Put on a large T-shirt that reaches at least to your knees. Tie a piece of string round your waist as a belt. Then ask a friend to help you put your toga on.

4. Togas were also worn in different ways, other than the pictures below. Remember, even the Romans found this difficult, so don't worry if you need to practise!

A SOLDIER'S LIFE

To conquer new lands for the empire and to keep the peace there afterwards, the Romans needed a large and skilful army. As the empire grew, the army became more and more important.

Controlling a huge number of soldiers is difficult. The Romans divided their army up into smaller groups of soldiers.

A century was a group of one hundred men, led by a centurion.

Each century was part of a cohort. Usually there were six centuries in a cohort.

Ten cohorts made up a legion. That is why soldiers were called legionaries.

In Roman times there were no trucks or aeroplanes to take soldiers to the farthest parts of the empire. They had to walk there carrying all their equipment. To make these journeys quicker and safer, the Roman army built thousands of miles of road all over the empire. These roads were so well made that some of them can still be seen today.

Most soldiers were infantry — they fought on foot. But there were also some horsemen, or cavalry, who were used for riding on ahead of the army to find the enemy.

Soldiers wore tunics and leather sandals. Over this they wore armour made of leather and metal. The armour had to be strong enough to protect them, but fairly light so that they could march long distances in it. Most soldiers carried spears and shields made of wood and leather. In colder parts of the empire, soldiers also wore woollen cloaks and leggings.

In training, soldiers practised forming different fighting groups. One of these was called a *testudo*, or "tortoise", — perhaps you can see why. It was useful if the enemy were throwing rocks or spears down from the walls of a fortress.

When they were attacking a walled city, the Romans used a huge catapult, called an *onager*, to hurl huge rocks at the walls.

Some soldiers built forts and walls as well as roads. Hadrian's Wall, which runs across the north of England, was about 73 miles long. It marked the most northerly border of the Roman Empire and made it easier to defend against Scottish tribes.

Legionaries came from all over the empire. Their lives were hard and they were often away from their families for years at a time.

There was always a danger that they would become fed up and rise up against their leaders. The emperors tried to keep them happy by paying them well and giving them a gift of money or land when they retired after 20 or 25 years of service.

FAMOUS ROMANS

JULIUS CAESAR

Born in about 100 BC, Julius Caesar was a great soldier. He helped to conquer new land for the Roman Empire, including most of what is now France. He returned to Italy in 49 BC and became the most powerful man in Rome. Some senators thought he was *too* powerful. They murdered him on 15 March 44 BC.

EMPEROR AUGUSTUS

Augustus' real name was Octavian. He was the adopted son of Julius Caesar. After Caesar's death, Octavian took power with two other men. One of these was Mark Antony. Later, these two fell out and Antony was defeated in battle. Octavian ruled alone and was given a special title: Augustus. Augustus was a clever and fair ruler who took account of the people's needs, but kept a tight control on everything. He was such a good emperor that when he died in AD14, the people did not want to go back to a republic.

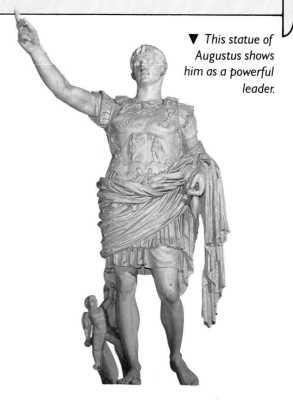

▼ *This statue of Augustus shows him as a powerful leader.*

▶ *This head of Claudius was found in a river in Suffolk, England.*

EMPEROR CLAUDIUS

Because he was often ill when he was young, Claudius led a quiet life, studying and writing history, until he was 51. Then he was made emperor because he was the only member of his family left. Although he was in some ways a strange choice, he ruled wisely until his death in AD 54. During his reign, Britain became part of the empire.

EMPEROR CONSTANTINE

After AD 305, the Roman Empire was split into an eastern empire and a western empire. Constantine the Great, as he was known, managed to unite the empire again for a while. He was the first emperor to become a Christian. He moved the capital of the empire from Rome to a new city in what is now Turkey. He called it Constantinople. Today we know it as Istanbul.

MAKE A ROMAN STATUE

Powerful Romans had statues of themselves set up in public places so that people would remember them. In Roman times, these statues were often painted in gold and bright colours, but the colours have since faded and today we only see the colour of the stone.

You will need: a one-metre piece of plastic-covered wire ● some plasticine ● wallpaper paste ● cotton wool ● cotton material ● pencil ● scissors ● wool or string ● poster paint.

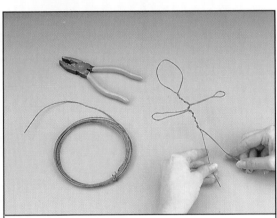

▲1. To make a wire skeleton for your statue, first fold the piece of wire in half. Then bend and twist the wire to make a figure like the one in the picture.

2. Mix the wallpaper paste with water to make a fairly stiff paste. Tear or cut some of your material into strips, dip them in the glue, and then wind them round your wire skeleton. You can put some cotton wool round the wire to make the head and stomach fatter.

3. Before the paste dries, bend the statue's arms and head into the right positions for your statue.

4. Cut a strip of material as long as your statue, but not too wide. Make a hole in the middle, dip it in the paste, and slip it over the statue's head. Overlap the sides and tie a piece of wool or string round your statue's waist.

5. Now spread out the rest of your material and draw a half-circle on it. The straight edge should be about three times as long as your statue. This is the statue's toga. Cut out the half-circle and dip it in the paste. Then drape the toga around your statue. Look at page 22 to see how to do this.

6. Make a mound of plasticine and push the legs of your statue into it. Leave it somewhere warm to dry until the paste has set hard. Then paint your statue.

THE END OF THE EMPIRE

Keeping order in the huge Roman Empire was always difficult. Many conquered people were unhappy under Roman rule and tried to rebel. The Roman army was kept busy acting as a police force throughout the empire. But problems came from *outside* the empire too. The Romans called people from beyond the empire barbarians. The barbarians were always attacking the borders of the empire, especially from the north.

By AD 300, the Romans had divided the empire in an attempt to control it better. One emperor ruled the western empire from Rome, while another emperor ruled the eastern empire from Constantinople. But all the time barbarians were attacking the borders and invading further and further into the empire. The Romans could not defend themselves on all sides at once.

In AD 455, Rome itself was seized by the barbarians, and just over 20 years later a German leader took over from the last western emperor. Strangely, this last emperor's name was a reminder of the very first days of Rome. It was Romulus Augustulus.

The eastern empire lasted much longer. It became known as the Byzantine Empire and kept many Roman customs and the Christian religion. But the eastern empire ended too, in 1453, when it was conquered by the Turks and became Muslim.

DID YOU KNOW?

SCRAPING, NOT SOAPING!

The Romans did not have soap. Instead, they covered their bodies with oil and then scraped the oil off with a special tool called a *strigil*. Dirt and dead skin came off with the oil. Rich people had a slave to do the scraping for them!

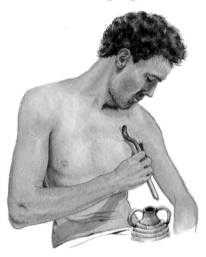

THE ROMAN CALENDAR

Our calendar is based on the Roman one. Like us, they had 365 days in a year, a leap year every four years, and twelve months. Here are the names of the Roman months. Do they look familiar?

Januarius
Februarius
Martialis
Aprilis
Maius
Junius
Julius
Augustus
September
October
November
December

LATIN WORDS

post scriptum means "after writing" — a PS is something you add after you have finished writing a letter.

nota bene means "note well" — NB is used to point out something important.

ante meridiem (am) means "before noon" — morning in other words! You can guess what *post meridiem* (pm) means.

ROMAN NUMBERS

Although the Romans were brilliant engineers, they were less good at maths! This was because they used a system of numbers that were very awkward to do sums with. You can still sometimes see Roman numerals on clocks or sundials.

1	I
2	II
3	III
4	IV
5	V
6	VI
7	VII
8	VIII
9	IX
10	X
11	XI
12	XII

Can you see which two months were named after famous Roman leaders? Page 26 will give you a clue.

GLOSSARY

Abbreviation — A short way of saying or writing a word.

Amphitheatre — A building in which shows were put on. It was usually built in a circle. Rows of seats rising around the space for the shows in the middle meant that everybody could see.

Amphorae — Pointed pottery jars for holding wine or oil.

Archaeologist — Someone who finds out about the past by looking at the buildings and objects that people have left behind.

Atrium — The hallway of a house, often open to the sky.

Barbarian — The Roman name for anyone who did not live in the Roman Empire.

Bulla — A lucky charm hung around the neck of a baby.

Cavalry — Soldiers who fought on horseback.

Centurion — Leader of a century.

Century — A group of 100 soldiers in the Roman army, led by a centurion.

Chariot — A cart with two wheels, pulled by horses.

Cohort — A group of about 600 soldiers in the Roman army.

Consul — A ruler in the time of the Roman republic. There were usually two consuls, who were in charge of the army and the laws.

Democracy — A country in which the people vote to decide who should be their leaders.

Emperor — The ruler of the Roman Empire.

Forum — The main square of a Roman town, where business was done.

Gladiator — A man (usually a slave) who was made to fight in a show to entertain people.

Infantry — Soldiers who fought on foot.

Legion — A group of nearly 6,000 soldiers, or legionaries, in the Roman army. A legion was made up of six cohorts.

Mosaic — A picture or pattern made of many small pieces of stone set in plaster.

Palla — A large shawl worn by Roman women.

Papyrus — A kind of paper made from reeds pressed together.

Pestle and mortar — A mortar is a strong bowl in which spices and other food can be crushed into a powder. The pestle is like a very heavy stick that pounds the food.

Republic — A country where the people choose their own leaders.

Senator — A member of the senate, which was the body of men who gave advice to the consuls during the Roman republic.

Slave — A person who had no rights in Roman times. Slaves were owned by their masters but were sometimes given their freedom.

Stola — A long dress worn by Roman women.

Stylus — A pointed stick for writing on a wax tablet.

RESOURCES

BOOKS TO READ
There are many good books on the Romans. Your library may have some of the following:

Roman Forts by Margaret Mulvihill. Franklin Watts 1990.

Rome by Simon James. Franklin Watts 1987.

The Romans by Anthony Marks and Graham Tingay. Usborne 1990.

The Roman World by Mike Corbishley. Kingfisher Books 1986.

Ancient Rome in association with the British Museum. Dorling Kindersley 1990.

PLACES TO VISIT
There are traces of the Romans in many parts of Britain. Ask at your library or Tourist Information Centre if there is anywhere nearby that you can visit.

British Museum
Great Russell Street
London, WC1B 3DG
Tel: 071 580 1788
The museum is open from Monday to Saturday, 10 – 5 and Sunday 2.30 – 6. It has beautiful Roman objects from many areas of Britain and other parts of the Roman Empire. Your local museum may well also have some Roman finds.

Roman Army Museum
Carvoran
Greenhead
Carlisle, CA6 7JB
Tel: 06977 47485
The museum is at Hadrian's Wall and is open every day from March to October, 10 – 5 (later in the summer), and Saturdays and Sundays from November to February, 10 – 4.

Corinium Museum
Park Street
Cirencester, GL7 2BX
Tel: 0285 655611
The museum is open from Easter to October, Monday to Saturday, 10 – 5.30 and Sunday 2 – 5.30. Cirencester was an important Roman town and the museum has full-size reconstructions of a Roman dining-room, kichen and mosaic workshop.

Roman Bath and Museum
The Pump Room, Abbey Churchyard
Bath, Avon
Tel: 0225 461111
The Roman baths at Bath were heated naturally by a hot spring. A temple has also been discovered and the museum shows many interesting Roman remains.

INDEX

Additional photographs: The Ancient Art and Architecture Collection 12(b), 20(both);
C.M. Dixon 5, 12(t), 14(b), 26(both); Michael Holford 14(t), 16; Zefa 28.